Jewish Spirituality

BY
RABBI BERNARD S. RASKAS

KTAV PUBLISHING HOUSE, INC.
JERSEY CITY, NJ 07306

ISBN 0-88125-826-1

The thoughts in this volume were expressed
originally in an expanded form in my three
volumes *Heart of Wisdom* published by the
United Synagogue of America, © copyright
1962, 1979 and 1986 and are being reprinted
with their permission.

Printed in the United States of America

Published by
KTAV Publishing House, Inc.
930 Newark Avenue, Jersey City, NJ 07306
info@ktav.com, www.ktav.com
(201) 963-9524 Fax (201) 963-0102

Introduction

We live in the presence of spirituality. Spirituality is all around us and in us. Spirituality is a way of looking at the world, thinking about the world, experiencing the world.

Through the lens of spirituality we constantly see the miracle of existence and are inspired to live a meaningful life. In this way we understand that what we daily think and do does matter in the life of the universe. Even more, this approach gives us purpose and faith. It is a faith that strengthens us in adversity and helps us to keep our balance during good fortune.

Through the centuries, Jews have evolved a unique expression of the concept of spirituality. In Jewish literature, history, and other forms, they have expressed their view of spirituality.

The thoughts in this volume I expressed originally in an expanded form in my three volumes *Heart of Wisdom* published by the United Synagogue of America. I am grateful for their permission to use those books as a source for these writings. It is my prayer that those who read this volume will find inspiration, hope and comfort in their daily lives.

May spirituality be the condition of all with whom we share the precious gift of life.

Bernard S. Raskas
Saint Paul, Minnesota,
Jerusalem, Israel

The Faith Behind "Amen"

The Hebrew term for faith is *emunah*. *Emunah* is quickly recognizable in the more common form of *ahmayn* or *amen*. It was first used by Psalmists and is still part of the prayer structure of the religions of the western world.

When we say "amen," we are in fact affirming our faith in God. We are demonstrating our willingness to accept the ways of the world, even though at any given moment they may not be so pleasing. It is a willingness to suspend judgment until we have greater perception, greater experience and greater knowledge.

If one lives in good faith with God, one will accept all events as a part of life. It is no great feat to accept a relationship when it is easy and profitable. But it is something to fulfill the terms of a relationship when it taxes and wearies us. Faith on a full stomach may be simply contentment; but if you have it when you are hungry, it is genuine.

Wait for the Lord; be strong, take courage, and wait for the Eternal.

PSALMS 27:14

1

I Am A Hebrew

The special character of the Jew is the concern with preserving a direct relationship with God that stands as the focal point of all existence.

Consider, for example, that other faiths have their names compounded with a founder or savior: Buddhism is the religion of Prince Gautama Buddha; Christianity is based on the name of its founder. But Judaism refers simply to the religion of the Jew. The Jew fervently maintains that between humans and God there is no need for an intercessor. The relation between the moral world, the natural world, God, and humanities is one. There is but one God, the God of all people and all creation.

I am a Hebrew; and I fear the Lord, the God of heaven, who hath made the sea and the dry land.

JONAH 1:9

2

The Orderly Universe

We do not often pause to contemplate the fact that the order of the universe reveals the presence of God. The solar system is perfect in its arrangement; the sun rises and sets at its appointed hour; and in general nature functions with absolute precision. The discovery of miracle drugs is founded on research which in turn is based on fixed mathematical principles of an orderly universe. The precision and the power of the laws and forces of the universe daily declare the reality of an intelligent God.

The sensitive mind does not see a conflict between science and religion, but rather a cooperative effort in which each discipline helps the other; the scientific study of religion and the religious study of science can help us live better lives.

A little science estranges men from God,
Much science leads them back to the Almighty.
LOUIS PASTEUR

How Deep Are Your Roots?

Once a young student came to Rabbi Akiba and said, "Teach me about faith." Rabbi Akiba showed him a tiny sprout and said, "Pull it up." The young man did so quite easily. Then the sage told him to pull up a young sapling. The lad did it with just a little more effort. Then he asked the boy to remove a small shrub from the earth. With both hands the young man did so. Finally, the rabbi asked him to uproot a full-grown tree. The student pulled with all his might but could not even shake a leaf. And Rabbi Akiba said, "Just so, my son, is it with faith. If our roots are deep, if our religion is grown and mature, no one can uproot it. Remember this, your faith will always be as strong and as powerful as are your roots."

Roots demand cultivation and nurturing. Faith, in a similar manner, requires our constant tending through study, thought and periodic recommitment.

The stronghold of the wicked crumbles like clay,
But the root of the righteous bears fruit.

PROVERBS 12:12

Building Bridges

The Kaddish prayer is written in Aramaic. It has not one reference to death and yet it is the most significant prayer during mourning, *yahrzeit* and *yizkor*. Often before people recite the Kaddish there is anguish and disorientation. But as soon as we finish, we usually find a mood of relaxation and acceptance. It is not the content that is significant but the sounds, the rhythm and the attitude.

One of the purposes of religion is to help us during the crisis points of our lives. Birth, adolescence, marriage, illness and death bring fundamental changes. In order to bridge those changes we literally have to build bridges.

It is important to have forms that will provide us with the means of transition so that we can go peacefully through life.

Out of divine commandments and deeds we build our bridges.

SONG OF SONGS RABBAH 8:10

The Big Flash

Following the first atomic explosion in New Mexico, observers were discussing what had gone through their minds when the "big flash" came. Dr. J. Robert Oppenheimer thought of a line of Sanskrit: "I have become Death, Destroyer of worlds." But William L. Laurence, the science reporter for the *New York Times*, said quietly that he thought, "This is the kind of a flash when the Lord said, 'Let there be light.'"

Tomorrow at dawn there will flash the first light for the new day. People will gather to welcome the first daylight with prayer and contemplation. We have hope because of the light of love, understanding, mercy, and truth. This is the only true light that can illuminate our world with faith and confidence.

The Holy One, observed, "How long shall the world exist in darkness? Let the light enter!" And God said, "Let there be light."

GENESIS RABBAH, CHAPTER 1

Prayer Is Practical

Prayer relieves anxieties. Prayer gives us a sense of perspective, enabling us to measure our lives against a set of values. Prayer identifies us with our people. Prayer connects us with the vast resources of our tradition to help us deal both with failure and success. Prayer is an opportunity to voice our pain in times of sorrow and to express thanksgiving in moments of joy. The purpose of prayer is threefold: helping us to accept things as they are, maintaining a sense of balance, inspiring hope in the future.

Prayer helps us to help ourselves. It enables us to use the wisdom of the ages to our best advantage. We can truly say that prayer has practical consequences. It helps us to live more stable and tranquil lives.

If a person must travel on the highway, he should offer a threefold prayer: the regular prayer, a prayer for a safe journey, and a prayer for safe return.

MIDRASH HANEELAM

The Meaning of Courage

Moses has an experience at the Burning Bush and is given the charge of leading his people into freedom. The Bible records the reaction of the Hebrew slaves: "And they did not listen to Moses because of shortness of breath and hard labor" (Exodus 6:9).

However, one may interpret the verse: "They did not listen to Moses because of shortness of spirit." They didn't have faith in God, faith in Moses and, most important of all, faith in themselves.

Israel is no exception to this rule. Because the pioneers drained the swamps and fertilized the desert they were able to lay the foundation of a state. The following generations built on that foundation. The strength and success of Israel today flows from its citizens' and its supporters' faith in the face of seemingly insufferable difficulties.

If we want to achieve something worthwhile, we must be willing to have faith in ourselves despite setbacks and obstacles.

Courage is never to let your actions be influenced by your fears.

ARTHUR KOESTLER

Faith Is Not A Blindfold

Faith can never be a substitute for the responsibilities of life. Faith can only do so much and the rest must be accomplished by skill, training, work and study which, of course, are based on a faith in a good and provident God.

Faith is not something we believe in spite of the evidence; it is something we do in spite of the consequence. Faith tears the blindfold from our eyes and forces us to see injustice when we would prefer a life of ease. True faith does not permit us to remain complacent and calm in the face of evil.

Albert Schweitzer has expressed this simply: "No one may shut his or her eyes and think that the pain which is therefore invisible is non-existent. No one may escape responsibility."

Serving God and humankind, through the inspiration and instrument of faith, forces us to involve ourselves, to give of ourselves, and if need be to offer up our lives.

It is not incumbent upon you to complete the work, But neither are you free from doing all you possibly can.

AVOT 2:21

More Light And Less Heat

The roof of the *sukkah* must be made of leaves or branches, with openings wide enough so that one can see the light of the sun by day or the stars by night. No heat but plenty of light. Perhaps this is a way of telling us that we need less of the heat of anger and tension; more of the light of understanding and tolerance.

Tolerance is not an admission of weakness but a mark of strength. When a person is intolerant of other views, he is merely saying that he is afraid of exposing himself to the possibility that others might have some truth on their side. When we are strong in our faith we have no need to be apprehensive of those who disagree with us; we may even be able to say, "While my approach seems right for me, your way may be right for you."

If we develop tolerance, we can take the stresses of conflicting views with serene confidence.

A wise person's duty is to be scrupulously faithful to the religious laws of the country and not to abuse those of others.

JOSEPHUS

Trust Yourself

Maurice Friedman, the philosopher, described our contemporary needs well when he said, "What modern man needs is not 'faith' in the traditional sense of that term, but a life stance on which to stand and from which to go out and meet the ever-changing realities and absurdities of our technological age."

This is an important insight into our world today. We are staggered by the rapidity of events. It seems the rules of the game of life are always being changed. This constant revision sets us running off in all directions seeking the magic solution: gurus, cults, and charismatic leaders; only believe and ye will be saved.

But we eventually tire of these experiments. The solution to our problem, the ability to cope with our concerns, lies within our own way of life, in our very own hearts. We have to learn to trust our own traditions and our own best instincts.

Abraham, the first patriarch, drew moral force from himself and walked in righteousness by his own effort.

RASHI ON GENESIS 6:9

11

Keep Your Feet On The Ground

Judaism flourishes today because it has met the test of history. One of the reasons for Judaism's spiritual strength is that it has been exposed to every philosophical test and has stood its ground.

Mahatma Gandhi once said: "I want the cultures of all the lands to be blown about my house as freely as possible, but I refuse to be blown off my feet by any of them."

The modern American Jew, like this great Indian seer, must be open to all points of view while holding steadfastly to his or her own faith. We must help the many causes in our wider community, but we will first accept our responsibilities to the Jewish community. We will look at the changes wrought by modern life, but we will also look to the wisdom of the ages before we change our devotion to Jewish life.

The greatest honor I can give my children is love for our people, loyalty to self.

THEODOR HERZL

Time On Our Hands

The giant sequoia trees have endured for centuries. This is because they take a great deal of time to reach their full growth.

Similarly, we must understand that it takes time to develop *our* spiritual strength and to reach *our* maturity. Certain things simply cannot be hurried. It takes nine months to develop a healthy baby. There are twenty-four hours in a day and no force on earth can hurry or delay that cycle. It takes *shivah*, a full week, for a mourner to accept the fact of a death; *sheloshim*, a full month, to accept the loss; and *avaylut*, a full year, to adjust to the deep pain. And no pill or scheme can shorten these periods.

That is why we should have time on our minds rather than time on our hands.

The Hebrews affirm the reality and importance of time. To them, it was not an illusion, something from which one must escape, but something which must be redeemed.

JAMES PHILLIP HYATT

The Pillars Of Prayer

The heart of prayer is not how many words we say, but rather the spirit in which we say them. Prayer is not a marathon in which the one who has said the most is necessarily the one who has done the best. Nor is it a speech contest in which the one who pronounces the words the most clearly is the winner. Prayer is an edifice built on the pillars of sincerity, conviction and trust in God, people and the universe.

Prayer must rest on a faith and a firm conviction in its purpose and its value. We must believe what we say, we must believe what we pray—or our prayer becomes mechanical, if not downright hypocritical.

My words fly up; my thoughts remain below:
Words without thoughts never to heaven go.
                    WILLIAM SHAKESPEARE

Tomorrow Is Only A Day Away

Commenting on the verse "Taste and see that the ways of the Lord are good" (Psalms 34:9), the rabbis ask how it is possible for everything we experience to be good. Their answer is that it is in our power to find something positive in everything that happens to us. We must make up our minds that events and encounters in the coming year will make us stronger, wiser, more caring, more loving human beings. No matter what befalls us, we must have faith—faith in ourselves and in tomorrow.

Today is merely a bridge to tomorrow.

FRANZ ROSENZWEIG

As Old As The Hills

The Jewish experience is as old as the hills. This implies stability and strength, knowledge and wisdom, faith and reassurance. Psalm 121, one of the oldest Psalms, was probably written by a Jewish pilgrim thousands of years ago as he approached the Hills of Judea. He looked forward to visiting the Temple in Jerusalem and he prayed: "I lift up my eyes to the hills [and I ask,] 'What is the source of my help?' My help comes from the Lord, Creator of heaven and earth."

It behooves us to remember the grandeur of the universe and the possibilities the Creator has bestowed upon us. We ought to recall the rhythms of nature and the fact that there are ebbs and flows in the affairs of people as well. Anxiety is inevitable. We must not act as if we were immune to all the fear and trembling that is a natural part of the human condition. God does not ask us not to feel anxious, but to trust in the Almighty no matter how we feel.

Faith is devotion to God.

JACOB JOSEPH KATZ

The Source Of Light

Jacques Lipschitz, the sculptor, spent his youth in Paris. One day a painter complained that he was dissatisfied with the light he painted and went off to Morocco, seeking a change. He found that the light in his Moroccan canvases was no different. Lipschitz then told him, "An artist's light comes from within, not from without."

Even as we are all artists in life, we must strive to kindle the light within. All that we touch and feel only serves as a stimulus. The true creative spark lies within our heart and soul.

We must learn to kindle our inner spiritual light. We can do this by developing the ability to trust ourselves and our own judgments. The nurturing of the inner spiritual fire is a lifetime enterprise. We must follow that light wherever it leads us.

The light of a candle is serviceable only when it precedes one on the way, useless when it trails behind.

BAHYA BEN ASHER

Save This

The seventh day of the festival of Sukkot is known as Hoshana Rabbah, "the great saving." Yom Kippur is the day of atonement, but so great is the compassion of God that if there are any sins left to be forgiven they can be redeemed on Hoshana Rabbah. It is a way of saying that the gates of mercy are never closed.

The principle behind Hoshana Rabbah represents a very important insight into human nature. We do not suddenly turn over a new leaf. It takes time and patience to develop a new orientation and to withdraw from old habits. Hoshana Rabbah is highly realistic. It says to us: Never despair. If you took two steps forward yesterday and you fell one step back today, you are still ahead by one. A mistake is only a mistake, it is not the final defeat.

Open the door of repentance only the width of the eye of a needle and God will open it wide enough for carriages and wagons to pass through.

SONG OF SONGS RABBAH, CHAPTER 5

18

No Comparison

Whenever we think of God, we must be aware that we are exploring a mystery; and when we have exhausted our thought, we have moved but one small fraction closer to comprehending God. Our lifetime is as a split second against the earth's eight billion years. We stand upon approximately two square feet in a universe that is described by a number with twenty-four ciphers in it. We grow humble and begin to perceive that we are but specks of dust.

Such thoughts stir us greatly. How, we wonder, can an individual stand on the hills and gaze at the stars, walk by the seashore and hear the endless pounding of the surf, look at a newborn infant and not understand that there is a God? And what that God thinks of us is far more important than what we think of God.

To whom will you liken God?
And to what can you compare the Eternal.

ISAIAH 40:18

19

It's Risky

Faith means risking. Faith means trust in God and ourselves. Ultimately faith is something we do in spite of the consequence.

If we have an ideal or a value and if we are willing to keep faith with it, we will eventually achieve something fine, glowing and wondrous. It could be in a career or in a business. It could be in a cause for others. But the important thing to realize is that our achievement will be tested by the depth of our faith. The challenge comes not in the beginning when it is easy but in the middle when it is tedious and difficult. But those who believe in themselves and their values will find that the risk was worthwhile.

Faith is not a series of theorems but a way of life.

SHMUEL HOGO BERGMAN

The Pillars Of Prayer

The heart of prayer is not how many words we say, but rather the spirit in which we say them. Prayer is not a marathon in which the one who has said the most is necessarily the one who has done the best. Nor is it a speech contest in which the one who pronounces the words the most clearly is the winner. Prayer is an edifice built on the pillars of sincerity, conviction and trust in God, people and the universe.

Prayer must rest on a faith and a firm conviction in its purpose and its value. We must believe what we say, we must believe what we pray—or our prayer becomes mechanical, if not downright hypocritical.

My words fly up; my thoughts remain below:
Words without thoughts never to heaven go.
WILLIAM SHAKESPEARE

You Are More Than You Are

We often wonder what effect our conduct and our religious faith have upon others. An interesting example can be found in a true story gleaned from the Talmud.

Simeon, the son of Shatah, sent his pupils to buy a camel from an Arab. When they brought him the animal, they gleefully announced that they had found a precious jewel in its collar. "Did the seller know of this?" he asked. When they said he did not, Simeon retorted, "Return the gem to the Arab immediately."

When the heathen received it he exclaimed, "Blessed be the God of Simeon ben Shatah. Blessed be the God of Israel!" This exclamation was dearer to Simeon than all the riches of the world.

In everything we say and do, we must remember that to others we represent the living image of our faith.

A person is always responsible for one's actions, whether awake or asleep.

BAVA KAMMA 3b

The Antidote To Anger

Often we are caught in the snare of the old adage that we must fight fire with fire. We retaliate against hate with hate, and we answer anger with anger. All we really succeed in doing is magnifying the problem.

The true way to extinguish a fire is with cool water. Likewise, the effective way to quench a quarrel is with cooling and soothing words. Most arguments are rooted in irrational hate; before reason can be applied to relationships, hate must be dispelled. This can only be done when the voice is soft, the temper is low, and the regard for others is gentle. The real antidote to anger is, obviously, pleasantness.

A soft answer turneth away wrath.

PROVERBS 15:1

23

Know-How

It is important to understand where people are coming from before we jump to conclusions. So often we justify ourselves while being critical of others. They are angry, we have righteous indignation. They are soft, we are forgiving. They are hypocrites, we compromise. All of this is a function of the way we perceive people and the context in which we operate.

As Jews this observation is most relevant. Being an Orthodox, Reform, or Conservative Jew does not require polemics or defensiveness. Each of us, in the context of our own experience, intellect, and personality, feels more comfortable in a given expression of Judaism. But we are all Jews.

We should be patient; truth may be seen from different perspectives, there is more than one way to interpret an event. That is why judgment should be restrained, balanced, and always made in context.

Without understanding there is no knowledge; without knowledge there is no understanding.
                                                           AVOT 3:17

24

To Whom Do You Belong?

Love is the most important word in the English vocabulary, and when it connects two people it is the most beautiful word as well. Love involves not just two people but a family and a community and, hopefully, the whole world. It means a sense of belonging, deep caring, and commitment in a totality of feelings.

The month of Elul precedes the High Holydays. The rabbis of the Talmud said that Elul is a mnemonic for a verse in the Song of Songs: *ani le-dodi ve-dodi li*—I belong to my beloved and my beloved belongs to me. While this refers to the relationship between God and human beings, it also describes the relationship that should exist among all creatures. And the finest expression of love is reflected in its durability and stability and compatibility.

What is love? The encircling and the joining of hearts together.

MIVCHAR HAPENINIM

Be Confident

Only the past do we know. In the classic code of Jewish law, the *Shulhan Arukh*, in the section known as *Yoreh Deah*, we find: "One should not consult astrologers, nor should one cast lots to determine the future." The future is unknowable, and in no way can we divine it. However, we can help shape it. There is such a phenomenon as self-fulfilling prophecy. If we are open, positive and hopeful, we can greet whatever may be, so that it will yield us its maximum benefits.

We must be optimistic. Why look for the worst when we can hope for the best? Why be anxious when we could just as well be affirmative? Why not take every step with confidence, with assurance, with trust?

Confidence is half the victory.

PERETZ SMOLENSKIN

Human Beings Are Different

It is always individual difference that accounts for the advances in human achievement. In fact, the Jewish tradition includes the blessing: "Praised are You, our God, Ruler of the universe, Who has created each person different."

In the Jewish view, every human being is unique. Locked up in each person is a storehouse of opportunity, of ability, of achievement, but only the individual can decide how to use this potential.

Beethoven wrote his magnificent symphonies alone because a board of directors never composed music. Shakespeare wrote his great plays alone because a committee cannot create literature. Freud made his momentous discoveries alone because a consensus never achieves breakthroughs in creative thinking. These are just a few examples of individual differences that help to make our lives more meaningful and more profoundly human.

If one sees a great crowd, one should thank God for not having made them all of one mind. For just as each person's face is different from another, so is each person's mind different from any other mind.

BERAKHOT 58a

27

Remember The Helper

A library becomes a library only when people take out books. A school is just a building until teachers and students enter and learning takes place. A synagogue is only a structure unless people come and worship.

All these examples indicate the great potential that we can discover in the world if we know how to relate to it properly. In a sense we are partners of God in the constant process of creating a better and more beautiful world.

Our job is to help God, our faith, our families, and our friends. The world is filled with the promise of greater and better things, but it is up to each of us to help realize this potential.

It was beautifully put by the late Rabbi Joshua Loth Leibman when he said, "Carbon atoms form charcoal when related in one way and become diamonds when related in another."

Whoever would change people must change the conditions of their lives.

THEODOR HERZL

Never Say "Never"

All of science, all of music, all of art, all of travel, all of literature, all new discoveries and adventure happen when people forget the words "impossible" and "never."

The importance of never saying "never" carries over into our personal lives as well. All of us face daily challenges that seem impossible and problems that appear insurmountable. But, the point is that while at the moment they may appear so, in the long run they really are not so. What must be remembered is that our action and our ability to solve problems is shaped by our attitude. For once we think we can't do it, we cannot. And if we are convinced we are unable to resolve a situation, we are finished before we start. That is why in viewing the challenges in our lives one should never say "never."

Restriction by others chains the mind; by oneself, paralyzes it.

LUDWIG BORNE

For Whom Do You Work?

According to popular belief success is determined by drive and is measured by how much one produces or owns. Business is worshipped as God; the office or plant becomes the House of God; the calculator replaces the liturgy; the closing of the financial books represents Judgment Day. And the sacrifices: they are merely family, friends, and self.

Be honest. For whom do you drive, run, amass?

Is there any widow living on the benefits of a good insurance policy and investments who would not take in washing if she could only have her husband back?

Why is it so hard to get a person to leave work for just a half hour for the welfare of a child? Money can be had every day, not so the child.

Why is it that when lifelong friends become partners, their money relationships can turn them into bitter enemies?

For whom do you work?

For whom do I work during the best part of my years and thereby deprive my soul of goodness and contentment?

JUDAH LEIB GORDON

Do You Understand?

Think for a moment how understanding might change your feelings.

Look at your boss and try to see what makes him act the way he does. Or study your employees and ask what makes them behave as they do. Observe children at play. What do they do and say? What are they trying to tell us?

Consider carefully a person who is tense. What produces tension in our lives? What relieves it?

Open your newspaper and ask yourself why people hate and kill when they seem to have everything. But do they have everything? What is "everything?" What do they lack?

Understanding does not come easily. Yet it is the only passkey to the mysteries of the world.

I shall light a candle of understanding in your heart which shall not be put out.

II ESDRAS **14:25**

31

Let There Be Peace

The Jewish tradition has taken great pains to strip war of glamor.

Moses had to conduct several wars to bring the Jews to the Promised Land. Yet he is not known as Moses the Warrior but rather Moses our Teacher. In Judaism, education is more important than fighting.

To unite Israel David conducted many military campaigns, yet he is not David the Conqueror but David the Sweet Singer of Israel. In Judaism, poetry is more important than battles.

During the time of Maccabees, the Rabbis chose not a war chant but a verse from Zechariah to celebrate military victory: "Not by power nor by might but by My Spirit says the Lord of Hosts."

Shalom, peace, is the value for which we should strive. That is why the important *kaddish* prayer ends: "May the One who makes peace in high places bring peace to all of us here."

Among other nations the vital problems are: a good crop, extension of boundaries, strong armies, colonies; among us, if we wish to be true to ourselves, the vital questions are: conscience, freedom, culture, ethics.

ISSAC LEIBUSH PERETZ

Leftover Turkey

The real test of a good cook is not what is served on Thanksgiving Day, but how the leftover turkey is handled. This test of how we handle life's leftovers is one we all must face. It is no feat to enjoy life's Thanksgiving days. The real test comes when life strips us bare as a Thanksgiving bird. How do we act on the day after? How do we conduct ourselves?

Each of us will someday be handed leftovers in life. There will be weeks of illness, days of grief, and moments of loneliness. Will we take what we have left over from the experiences of good times to help us live through difficult times? This all depends on whether you know the recipe for leftover turkey.

Grant me the serenity to accept the things I cannot change, courage to change the things I can and wisdom to know the difference.

REINHOLD NIEBUHR

The Staff Of Life

While it is important to have certain necessities, we must never forget that the basic satisfactions in life do not derive from bread alone. Unless we constantly restock our mental storehouses, we will find our lives insignificant.

When we cease to use our brains, we cease to exist. We are more than breathing organisms or workhorses. We are creatures who marvel at the wonders of the world and constantly seek to express feeling about the universe. There are books to read, theaters, films and art shows to attend, politics and problems to work at, places to visit. All these can help us stretch our minds and our souls so that we continually experience a sense of growth. We generate enthusiasm and acquire satisfaction that far exceed the pleasure of acquiring material things. While it is important to have a full stomach, it is just as important to have a full mind.

For one does not live by bread alone.

DEUTERONOMY 8:3

34

Person To Person

One of the great purposes of law is to protect people, to help the individual, and to preserve not only the sacredness but the welfare of each human life. The importance of every person is an unchanging, eternal fact of life as well as of religion. People are the ultimate values in this world; everything else comes second.

No matter who we are, where we are, or what we do, it is the person that should determine our thoughts and our actions. Almost every undertaking in this world could be improved if we would be aware that we are dealing not with things or decisions or programs but rather with persons.

We should struggle to maintain this awareness in our technological society, which tends to obliterate the person. All of us tend to forget that the essential purpose of living is to make ourselves truly human.

The welfare, right, and honor of every individual, even the lowest, is the community's concern.

FRIEDRICH J. STAHL

The Vital Balance

The Book of Ecclesiastes sums up life (3:11): "The Creator has made everything beautiful in its own time."

At birth there is the pain of delivery but also the pleasure of a new child. In infancy there are illnesses and long hours. But there is also the joy of the first words and the bright, happy moments.

School means schedules and worries and anxieties. But then comes the exhilaration of the *Bar* and *Bat Mitzvah*.

Adolescence can be frustrating and infuriating. But if we can help a young person through this very difficult period, we find our lives really endowed with meaning.

And then there is marriage with its possibilities and its problems. And middle age and old age and even the last peaceful relief to be found in death.

We are all subject to certain demands which at times seem beyond us. But if we have a vision of life's larger purposes, we will learn to say yes to life and even learn to appreciate every age and stage.

Balance the loss caused through a good deed versus the gain, and the gain through a sin versus the loss.

AVOT 2:1

Learning Laughter

Joy and laughter are indispensable to emotional and spiritual well-being. To make others laugh is a talent, but to be able to laugh ourselves is as necessary to living as air is to breathing.

Humor, when properly used, is a means of lessening personal hostility and of dispelling self-hatred. Moreover, laughter is often effective in expressing the truth. We can often say in jest the things we would not dare to express directly. In situations of emotional tension, humor frequently helps those involved to gain the perspective they need to look at the situation realistically.

The person who can laugh with life has developed deep roots within the soil of faith. The conviction that one's personal existence has meaning gives one the deep serenity that makes living a real joy. From this joy comes the strength to meet and resolve life's problems.

In laughter the pain of the heart is eased.
PROVERBS 14:13

Good Timing

Are there any guidelines that can help us live a stable and satisfying life? There always will be factors beyond our control: social forces, illness, developments in the economy. We cannot determine how long we will live or how our children turn out. Our influence over the future—indeed, over the present—is necessarily circumscribed.

If we are to find peace of mind we must accept the facts of life. What we cannot cure, we must learn to endure. Worrying will not change the realities. But prayer can help us see things in the proper perspective. In Jewish theology there is no room for self-pity or despair.

On the contrary, Judaism maintains that, despite appearances, things can work out for the best. Misfortune may turn out to be good fortune. What once was loss turns out to be gain. To ensure our emotional and spiritual well-being, we must cultivate patience, perspective and a sense of proportion.

Time is the most sublime and wisest teacher.

MOSES IBN EZRA

Individuality

The Talmud tells us that every person is supposed to say, *bishvili nivra ha-olam*, "For my sake was the world created." Each of us must feel our own uniqueness, each of us must develop an individual personality, each of us must find the special reason for being created.

All of us have had the experience of shopping for a garment. There are times when we try it on and the salesperson says, "That's really you."

In the same way we should be able to get up every morning and look in the mirror and say, "That's really you." Because in a real sense the world was made for you and you were made for the world.

A human being is not a cypher, but a living creature. . . . a whole world and a part of the world as well . . . a closed world and an open world no less.

DAVID BEN-GURION

The Chain Of Love

Love is not a divisible thing. It is rather a chain reaction that leads us on to higher forms. We fall in love with a stranger, and then we marry the stranger and the stranger becomes our spouse. Then through the love of another person, we learn how to love a family. From the love of family we come to learn love for a community. From the love of a community, we reach the stage of a love for the world. Then in and through the love of the world, we learn to love God. By the first act of love of one person, we eventually bring God and the world together. This is not something we do accidentally but in a positive, deliberate way. We must choose before we can begin to love.

The classic statement on love for others (Leviticus 19:18) is "Love thy neighbor as thyself, I am the Lord." There we have stated the proper order and choice. We should love human beings before God. But true love of God begins with the love of people.

The love of people is at the same time a love for God. For when we love one, we necessarily love one's handiwork.

JUDAH LOEW

The Ultimate Honesty

There is a beautiful saying that should be engraved on our hearts. The Rebbe of Kotzk once noted that a truly religious person is "one who goes beyond the letter of the law." He pointed out that according to the letter of the law, one should be honest in dealings with others. But a thoroughly honest person goes beyond the letter of the law, not only being honest with others but with her- or himself as well.

It is a kind of spiritual dishonesty that makes us scan the faces of a social set cringingly, searching for approval. Does the need for acceptance by others blind us to the fact that God gave us intelligence to think for ourselves?

It is important to a life of honesty to do what is right in the eyes of God and our conscience, not in the eyes of our neighbors. A life of honesty is achieved by a person who is less concerned with being socially acceptable and more concerned with being spiritually accountable.

And thou shalt do what is good and right in the eyes of thy God.

DEUTERONOMY 12:28

Priceless

Many of us mistakenly believe that the true worth of a gift is measured in terms of monetary value. We think that the more expensive the gift, the more regard or affection it shows. This is a fallacy, for love cannot be bought and friendship cannot be purchased. In time all material things must perish and vanish. What we ourselves do for others—what we give of our thoughts, our energies, our consideration—this truly expresses our devotion.

The expression of personal concern and interest makes the kind of impression on memory that time cannot erase nor circumstances alter. When we give something of ourselves, we have planted a seed of friendship that will bear fruit continually.

God desires the heart.

SANHEDRIN 106 b

Inside Out

There is a *midrash,* teaching, connected with nuts that has a serious message: "It is the characteristic of a nut that no matter how much dirt or mud falls on it, once it is washed and cleaned, the inner fruit is edible" (Shir Hashirim Rabbah 6:17).

Clearly, we interpret this in terms of Jewish history. No matter what happened, no matter how much abuse and suffering our enemies heaped upon us, we maintained our integrity. When we walked into our homes, our synagogues and Houses of Study, we washed away the vile slanders, the hatred, the discrimination. We found refuge in our Bible; our Talmud, our prayer book, and faith gave us the strength and courage to endure and survive. That is why we can approach the 21st century with honor and with pride.

This applies to us as a people and as individuals. If we can maintain our sense of worth, we will ultimately triumph over life's inevitable trials and tribulations.

The roads to freedom do not run through the lands out yonder, but rather through our inner selves.

ARTHUR SCHNITZLER

The Three C's

Part of the reason we suffer so much in human relations is our unrealistic view of human nature. We tend to see and judge people in absolute terms, as if they had to be models of perfection. From the Jewish point of view, everyone is a mixed bag of emotions, capable of good and bad, aggression and passion, hate and love. Sometimes our controls may slip, our worst side comes out, and others are hurt. This is why we all need to forgive and to be forgiven.

How wise we would be if we would learn to get off each other's backs. Parents need not be excessively demanding, nor children overly provocative. If older people tend to press for more conformity, it is equally true that younger people are often insensitive and indiscriminate in condemnation and criticism.

We can recover a sense of peace and balance. We must learn the satisfaction that comes through the three C's—common sense, consultation and compromise.

Rabbi Joshua ben Korcha says: It is meritorious to compromise.

SANHEDRIN 6b

Changes

We are not today what we were yesterday; and what we were yesterday, we were not the day before. Physically, our entire organic structure replaces itself every seven years. In life itself, we are constantly changing our roles. One day we are children, soon we are adolescents, then spouses, parents, and so on up the ladder of life. If there be any fixed rule about life, it is that change and flux is its chief characteristic.

We must understand this basic rule of living and accept the changes within us as individuals and within society.

We must learn to taste to the fullest and enjoy to the utmost the present role we are enacting. It is a part assigned to us for a limited number of performances. Let us seize the moment, before change gives us another role in life.

The main business of a rational society is the business of living with change, comprehending it, and if possible, making it subordinate to the human situation.

NORMAN COUSINS

To Life

Life is everything. It is for this beyond all else that we pray and yearn. One of the most meaningful and heartfelt Jewish prayers is to be found in two simple Hebrew words: *zokhraynu lehayim,* "Remember us for life."

If we had a choice, it would be to continue another year. It is something we all want for our dear ones and ourselves. We hope and pray that this wish will come true for all of us. But whatever the future may hold, let us be content that we made it so far.

All that we have, we would give for life.

JOB **2:4**

No, Too, Is An Answer

There are certain things in which we can go only so far. We can go only so far in work and in play, in eating and in drinking, and even in grieving and mourning. We must understand that there are limits to everything we do in life. Learning to live with limits is learning to be mature. Understanding the words "no" and "not" is an important part of a good and wise life.

Learning the word "not" is an important religious experience.

We can unite in firm negation of idolatry and find perhaps more of a common faith in this negation than in any affirmative statement about God. Certainly we shall find more of humility and of brotherly love.

ERIC FROMM

The Dawn of Conscience

The first episode in the Bible that highlights clear moral choice and our accountability for our actions is the Cain and Abel story. God asks Cain, "Where is Abel, your brother?" Cain replies: "Am I my brother's keeper?" The answer of the Bible is that we *are* each other's keepers, for God's reply is: "The blood of your brother is crying out to Me." This phrase represents the first statement of conscience, and with it begins the history of civilization.

What all this is really telling us is that the way to lessen our anxiety is to accept moral responsibility. Biblical history specifically, and history generally, demonstrate that when we had faith in ourselves and lived by a set of moral values, we sustained ourselves and survived. For it is humaneness that can abolish our mutual anxieties. The Jewish conviction is that only conscience can save and secure a civilization.

Conscience is, like charity, a Semitic importation. Israel introduced it into the world.

ANATOLE LEROY–BEAULIEU

Priorities

A rabbi once asked: If one has to choose whether to serve people first or God, what should one do? He found the answer in the well-known verse in Leviticus 19:18, "You shall love your neighbor as yourself, I am the Lord."

The rabbis said: Notice the order of the phrases—first comes your neighbor and then comes God. If there is a conflict, then people are first.

The late and great Abraham Joshua Heschel pondered the rabbis' comments and then offered this observation: Every human being is made in the image of God. Therefore, if we are serving our fellow human beings, in a very real sense we are serving God as well. This is a very important insight into Jewish tradition, if not into all of religion.

The love of people is at the same time a love for God. For when we love one, we necessarily love one's handiwork.

JUDAH LOEW

On Justice

A major ingredient of a sound society is a passionate concern for justice. Indeed, the concept of justice may very well be the most important contribution of Judaism to Western thought. Justice is one of the great demands that the Biblical faith makes on us.

This zeal is summed up in Deuteronomy: *tzedek, tzedek, tirdof*—"Justice, justice shall you pursue." Rabbi Simhah Bunim, a Hasidic rabbi of the last century, was asked why the word "justice" was repeated twice. He answered: "This is to teach us that justice should be pursued only through justice. It can be established only through just means."

Ends do not justify means. To hurt some people in order to benefit others is abhorrent to Jewish tradition. As it has been said, "Justice is the passionate concern to wipe the tears from every face in the world"—which means that everyone is regarded as holy.

For the Lord of Hosts is exalted through righteousness, and God, the Holy One, is sanctified through justice.

HIGH HOLY DAY LITURGY

50

The Silent Chamber

In the ancient Temple there was a "Silent Chamber." It was so constructed that coins could be left there by one person and withdrawn by another without either party ever seeing the other. Thus, donor and recipient remained anonymous. Such a secret treasury existed in every town in ancient Israel. One purpose of the Silent Chamber was to ensure that the needy could receive gifts without any possibility of embarrassment. Another was to teach people that in the highest form of giving, the donor remains anonymous.

It would be a fine spiritual exercise for all of us to create our own equivalent of a Silent Chamber, to give without pride and conceit. The Silent Chamber would accomplish many purposes, for it would enable us to give without embarrassing the recipient.

Whoever gives anonymously is greater than Moses.

BAVA BATRA 9b

The Support of the Universe

The problems of cosmogony, the origin of the universe, and cosmology, the nature of the universe, have intrigued minds in all ages. What especially baffled human curiosity was how the earth and the universe were supported in space.

The Greeks believed the universe was supported by a powerful giant, Atlas. The Babylonians thought the earth floated in a vast, watery mist. The Egyptians assumed that it rested on a huge ball. The Hindus believed that it rested on a giant turtle.

The answer of the Hebrews, found in the Ethics of the Fathers, is both timeless and indispensable: "Rabban Simeon ben Gamaliel said, the world rests on three things: on truth, on justice, and on peace." The Jew looks at everything through eyeglasses focused by ethics and morality.

The three are really one, for when justice is done, truth prevails and peace is established.
JERUSALEM TALMUD, TAANIT 4:2

Act of God

One windy day a snow-laden telephone pole crashed onto the automobile of a Pennsylvania motorist. The car was damaged and its owner sustained injury. He sued the telephone company. The court awarded him $10,830, holding that the company was at fault because it had not inspected the pole for fifteen years. The court did not accept the company's claim that the pole fell because of an "act of God."

In cautioning us against using God as a scapegoat, the judge gave us an excellent lesson in theology. Though much of our life is determined by factors beyond our control, including chance and Divine Providence, yet in the moral universe we remain our own masters. We are free agents in determining how we shall use the elements of nature, how we shall deal with others, how we shall conduct our personal lives.

What belongs to God is God's; what belongs to humans is humanity's.

YIDDISH PROVERB

Humility Is Hard

In the entire order of the universe, it is important for a person to know his or her place. Often our technological achievements induce a false sense of importance. We forget that we are simply using the laws of nature and the universe; we do not own them, nor did we even make them. Human beings have reached the moon but were only specks of dust in comparison to its surface. If we remember this, then even with our fantastic accomplishments we will have a sense of humility. We will know that what we are comes from the world about us, and we will understand how dependent we are on the forces of nature and the labors of others.

This was well summarized by Albert Einstein: "A hundred times a day I remind myself that my inner and outer life depend on the labors of others, living and dead; and that I must exert myself in order to give in the same measure as I have received and am receiving."

Humility is a virtue which all preach, none practice, and yet everybody is content to hear.
                                          JOHN SELDEN

The Highest Degree

From the Jewish point of view, it is better than any academic title or degree to be called a *mensch*. Being a *mensch* means doing what is right, decent, and proper.

The greatest of all Jews had only one title: *ha-ish Moshe*, "the man Moses." He was a person who lived to do his duty, carry out his responsibilities, and have consideration for others.

Education may solve some problems, but it will create others unless it is education for *character*. Germany had the highest educational standards of any country and had made enormous contributions to scholarship. And what did the Germans do? They started the Second World War, bringing terror and genocidal destruction to millions of innocent victims. Our ancestors said it well: "Learning is good if it is joined with good character."

One who possesses both learning and character is like an artist with all tools at hand.

AVOT DE–RABBI NATAN 22

Everyone a Judge

The seventeenth verse of the twenty-fourth chapter of Deuteronomy tells us, "You shall not deny the rights of the stranger." And the Bible adds: "For you shall remember that you were a slave—a stranger—in the land of Egypt."

Here the Bible appeals to us to be careful of the rights of others not on the basis of a moral code nor even of a belief in God but rather of personal experience. This mode of thought, using one's own feelings as the basis of one's actions, can be very important. For example, when we criticize minority groups and their actions, have we forgotten how we felt when *we* were in the ghetto? We often are harshly critical of teenagers. Have we forgotten what it means to face all the dilemmas of growing? Very often we pass judgment on some act, forgetting that in a period of stress we once did the very same thing. All of this is implied in this Biblical verse.

The gateway to compassion is a passion for understanding.

SAMUEL M. SILVER

The Chain of Compassion

God desires all people to be filled with compassion and mercy. The Hebrew word *rachum* is the root of the Yiddish *rachmones*—a word that cannot really be translated. It means more than just being merciful. The closest we can come in English is the notion of compassion—knowing what it is like to be in another's shoes.

Each of us, every day, can find simple ways to be compassionate. By being just a little more thoughtful, we can bring more *rachmones* into the world. For what is the world but a machine unless we supply the human touch? What does it mean to be created in the image of God unless we reflect God's greatness? There is a chain reaction of mercy. Mercy begets more mercy, and compassion generates more compassion, and the chain reaches all the way to heaven.

Every time that you are compassionate, the Compassionate One shall have compassion upon you.

TOSEFTA BAVA KAMMA 9

A Kind of Loving

An important Jewish value is *chesed*, loving-kindness. This is the rare instance when the English translation accurately expresses the essential meaning of the Hebrew. For *chesed* is more than love and greater than kindness.

To raise your child is an act of love. But to bring a foster child into your home is loving-kindness.

To visit a member of your family who is institutionalized because of chronic illness is an act of kindness. But to visit someone in the same circumstances who is not even remotely related to you is an act of loving-kindness.

Loving-kindness means extending ourselves to become noble. It implies doing what is not required, performing a good deed simply because it is a part of our tradition to live with others in *chesed*, in loving-kindness. And it is what the world most needs.

The highest form of wisdom is loving-kindness.
BERAKHOT 17a

For Goodness Sake

It is important as we consider the many problems that beset our community to keep in mind that those who do the most significant work are not the critics but the creators. Those who truly serve God and humankind are those who find how to build, those who act out of compassion and a sense of justice rather than out of fear.

Some of us have the notion that we should only do things when we are threatened. This kind of motivation is negative and harmful. The real *mitzvah* is performed because it is the right thing to do. There are those who feel that we should help the poor in order to prevent social upheaval. But shouldn't we do this because it is right to help every citizen achieve liberty and a good life?

Let a good person do good deeds with the same zeal that an evil person does bad ones.

THE BELZER REBBE

Willing and Able

The more we study the background against which the Torah was given—Canaanite civilization and Semitic environment—the more we can appreciate the voluntaristic spirit of Judaism. The concept of *tzedakah* goes beyond the charity to embrace both individual involvement and communal responsibility.

The Bible requires us to leave "a corner of the field" for the poor, but it does not tell us exactly how much. The ancient Israelites were instructed to appear before God in Jerusalem three times a year and make an offering: "Everyone as able." The term *nidavah,* a *free-will* offering, occurs many times.

During the Middle Ages the Jewish communities of Germany and Poland administered their own affairs. There was no instrument to enforce the laws passed by the community council, but Jews complied freely. Generosity is an instinctive Jewish response.

If a person is occupied with the needs of the community, it is as though he or she were occupied with Torah.

JERUSALEM TALMUD, BERAKHOT 5a

Priest and Prophet

One of the most important Hebrew essayists of the twentieth century was Ahad Ha'am. In "Priest and Prophet," he discusses the contrast between the person of action and the person of vision.

The visionary and the implementer serve complementary functions, he points out. Without Aaron, Moses' mission would have failed. Aaron helped to cast Moses' ideals and dreams in a practical form. The tradition of Aaron stands for translating morality into reality.

Each of us contains a little of the visionary and a little of the practical. We must have high goals to inspire us, but we must be prepared to embody them in practical means. We must take the supreme values of peace, integrity, and humanity and make them operate daily.

Be of the disciples of Aaron, loving peace, pursuing integrity, and bringing humanity closer to the principles of the Torah.

AVOT 1:12

The Curse of Conformity

According to an ancient rabbinic legend which has its counterpart in Greek mythology, the people of Sodom had a special bed. Every visitor was placed in it. In order to pass through the city one had to fit the bed. If one's legs were too long, they were brutally shortened. If they were too small, they were stretched. The stranger had to conform to the measurements of society. For this cruelty—so goes the story—the city of Sodom was destroyed.

The habits of Sodom are not completely different from our own, for we, too, are expected to fit the bed, fit the social norm, or we are cut off.

The sin of forcing people into a certain mold not only hurts others but also retards our own possibilities of growth. By respecting individual thoughts and actions, we promote our own individual development as well.

The idea of liberty as evolved by the Anglo-Saxon mind signifies liberty of conscience, the full, untrammeled development of the soul as well as the body.

ISRAEL FRIEDLANDER

God Is One

The Jewish religion is solidly founded on belief in the unity of God. The first commandment requires us to recognize God's sovereignty. "I am the Lord your God . . . You shall have no other gods before Me." Every *berakhah*, blessing, begins with the traditional formula praising God as Ruler of the Universe. There is no Jewish God, no Christian God, no Moslem God, for God is above and beyond all theologies. There may be a Jewish, Christian, or Moslem approach, but these are merely ways to view God, to express feelings and thoughts. It is our privilege, indeed it is our right, to worship as we see fit.

Tragically, tolerance has not always prevailed. We Jews were the first people in history to fight (and die) for freedom of worship. We must continue this fight to protect the vital principles that are part of our heritage—as Americans and as Jews.

Hear, O Israel: The Lord our God the Lord is One.

DEUTERONOMY 6:4

63

The Value of One

In Jewish history, individuals have made momentous contributions. It was Moses whose thought and leadership saved the Jewish faith, and, indeed, the values of the civilized world. It was the Baal Shem Tov—one simple person, not even a rabbi—who started the Hasidic movement which changed the face of Judaism forever. In our own time it was a lady from Baltimore named Henrietta Szold who founded Hadassah, the movement dedicated to the healing of our people that has distinguished itself in service to Israel.

And what of the future? We know that individuals will come forward who will make the difference.

One person yelling "Fire!" in a crowded room can cause untold harm. One malicious rumor can ruin a reputation. One individual can make a difference.

One individual has the power to face thousands and to stand up to peoples and generations.

ISAAC LEIB PERETZ

The Dawn of a New Day

When Jews see the dawn break, they are obligated to recite the morning prayer. But when is the exact moment of daybreak? Some two thousand years ago, two rabbis debated this issue.

One declared: "The night ends and a new day begins when we can tell the difference between a blue thread and a purple thread."

The second said, "The night ends and the day begins when we can distinguish the face of our neighbor." In other words, when we can see our neighbor not as a blur but as a person with features and feelings.

What a sensitive insight! When we relate to people as human beings, unique and different, then a new relationship can begin. A new day will dawn for humanity when we all see our neighbors in this new light. That is why Rabbi Akiba declared that "You shall love your neighbor as yourself" was the most important verse in the Bible.

Humanity is a living organism, of which races and peoples are the members.

MOSES HESS

The Moral Equivalent of War

Our beliefs are fixed like stars in the sky to guide the course of our lives. The light of their teachings illuminates our conscience. They have never failed us. They are stated in the eloquent words of our tradition:

"Am I my brother's keeper?"

"You shall love your neighbor as yourself."

"Justice, justice shall you pursue."

"Nation shall not lift up sword against nation."

We are not merely preservers of a tradition, but are summoned to battle against a sea of troubles. We must assert ourselves against greed, corruption, oppression, and abuse of human beings.

Much of the despair of our public and private lives today is due to spiritual disorientation. Moral fatigue has set in because of the collapse of hallowed visions and clear ideals to which lives once were honor bound. To those visions and ideals we must return.

We are God's stake in human history.

ABRAHAM JOSHUA HESCHEL

The Challenge of Darkness

The evil of the world is great, but the power of good is also great. And the power of good is derived from many, many small deeds of goodness. The more individuals who share in the act of goodness the mightier it becomes. If we all will determine to do the very most we can to create a better world, we will really make it better. For as Goethe aptly put it. "If each person will sweep in front of his door, then the whole world will become clean."

Blessed is the match that is consumed
  in kindling flame.
Blessed is the flame that burns
  in the secret fastness of the heart.
Blessed is the heart with strength to stop
  its beating for honor's sake.

HANNAH SZENES

The American Spirit

What does America stand for? Concern for our fellow human beings. Compassion. Education and culture. Training people for jobs. Improving health care. Aiding refugees.

This is what the Bible is all about: sharing our bread with the hungry, freeing the oppressed, providing material, emotional, and spiritual support for people in need. The Bible teaches us to rise above involvement in self, to feel a sense of responsibility for others.

Elliot Richardson, the former Secretary of Health, Education and Welfare, gave this apt summation: "In concept, the ethic and the act of concern for the welfare of one's fellow human beings is . . . a very deep part of the Hebraic tradition. It is a foundation stone of the Judeo-Christian ethic. It is a particularly American quality."

Ours has become a nation too great to offend the least, too mighty to be unjust to the weakest, too lofty and noble to be ungenerous to the poorest and lowliest.

STEPHEN S. WISE

Thought Is Free

The Talmud is divided into two categories. One is *halakhah,* the code of religious-legal rulings that comprises our system of observance. The other is *aggadah,* anecdotes and adages, parables and proverbs that reflect the wide-ranging and diverse views of the sages. These views, unlike *halakhah,* are nonbinding: Later generations are free to accept, reject, or modify earlier views in light of the findings and the scientific thinking of their own age. Thus, while ethical conduct is mandated, freedom of thought is encouraged. Intellectual adventure has always been an important factor in Jewish life.

Intellectual honesty is not only a right but also a responsibility. This is basic to Jewish thought.

Thought is the world of freedom.

DOV BER OF MEZERITCH

In the End

Famous Last Words is an anthology of 2,500 exit lines. As one reads these final messages there is an obvious conclusion: an entire life is vastly more important than its last words, sublime as they may be.

This is an important lesson. Not what we say but what we do really matters—not the words we utter today but how we live tomorrow. The choice is always ours.

A passage in the Ethics of the Fathers puts it graphically: "The store is open and the storekeeper gives credit. The account book is open and the hand writes. Everyone who would borrow, let them come and borrow. But the collectors go round continually every day and exact payment with or without one's knowledge."

The world is a supermarket. We can choose what we want, but in the end we must pay the price.

You have fire and water before you, choose which you want. There are life and death before every person; what each wants will be given.
                              BEN SIRA 15:16–17

70

The Jew In You

Friedrich Wilhelm, the king of Prussia, once asked his chaplain to prove in one word the truth of religion. "Your Majesty," the chaplain replied, "the Jews."

He correctly saw that the Jews, collectively and individually, are the embodiment of a long and continuous history of religious ideas and teachings for which they have struggled throughout the ages.

Jews who live with a sense of history are aware of this identity, of themselves, of humanity, of their past, of their possibilities. The past is a foundation on which Jews must build if they would be loyal to those who have laid the spiritual foundations of Judaism.

It is a unique thing to be born a Jew. Ultimately, however, to be born a Jew is an accident, but to live as one is an achievement.

I am a Jew because for Israel we are not yet created; we are creating Israel.

EDMOND FLEG

Deeds Not Creeds

Rabbi Akiva said, "This is the greatest principle of Torah: 'And you shall love your neighbor as yourself'" (Jerusalem Talmud, Nedarim 9:4). Why does the Torah say "Love your neighbor" instead of all humanity? Clearly, the Torah avoids meaningless abstractions. It is relatively easy to love a starving child in India or an oppressed black in South Africa. That kind of "verbal love" does not cost much financially or emotionally. But it takes considerable effort to love neighbors when their garbage spills onto our lawn or their children trample our flowerbeds or their music shatters our eardrums. It requires great tolerance to coexist amiably with a neighbor whose outlook or lifestyle is opposed to ours.

Moreover, when the Torah enjoins us to love our neighbor, the focus is on people not on possessions. In the final court, all we leave behind us is the memory of the good we have done to others.

Good deeds are done by good people.

SHABBAT 32a

72

Sharing The Teachings

While the Torah was essentially written in the Hebrew language and was the direct responsibility of the Jewish people, it also has worldwide implications. The great concepts of morality, justice and peace all find their origins in the Bible. The Bible is now available in 1,232 languages and dialects. Yearly some 70 million copies are sold or given away.

Most of the events recorded in the Bible occurred in an area only 200 miles long and 80 miles wide. The tiny land of Israel has had a stunning impact on the manners and the morals of the whole world. What was given at Sinai and what was created in the land of Israel is a part of the human conscience. But it is not enough to take pride in this heritage; more important, we must share it. We must not only study the Bible regularly but make it available to all those who seek it.

The Torah was given publicly in the wilderness, in no one's land, so that Jews may understand its teachings are to be shared with others. Anyone wishing to accept it is welcome to it.

MEKHILTA TO EXODUS 19:2 יׂת

A Reminder

It takes money to buy wine; it takes wine to recite the Kiddush; it takes Kiddush to sanctify the Sabbath; and it takes the Sabbath to endow our week with a sense of meaning.

We need a regular, periodic reminder of the purpose we serve on this earth. This reminder cannot be left to chance, for what is left to chance often does not occur. The meaning of our lives is so important that Jews have embodied it in the ceremonial of the Sabbath, so that we are reminded at least once a week of the purpose of our creation and our existence.

In love and favor Thou hast given us the holy Sabbath as a heritage, a reminder of Thy work of creation, first of our sacred days.

SABBATH KIDDUSH

Oneness

An American woman lived with her husband on an African rubber plantation. One day a native boy asked, "When a white person sees God, has God a white face?" She answered with great care, "I would fear to look upon the face of God, but I will tell you what I think . . . I think the side of God's face that is in the sun will be bright, and the side toward the night will be dark, so that no one can say that the face of God is any color at all."

Like the face of God, souls are without color. We all tend to see God in terms of our own race and culture, but God is beyond the restrictions of a particular view. And God, in turn, sees unrestricted by race or a particular outlook. This idea unites us all as children of the one God.

It is important to make this oneness of humanity a part of our daily thought, but even more vital to make it a part of our natural way of life.

One was created the common ancestor of all so that the various families should not contend with one another.

SANHEDRIN 38 a

The Names Of God

In the book of Exodus (6:2-3) God speaks to Moses and says, "I appeared to Abraham, Isaac and Jacob as *El Shaddai*, God Almighty. However, by My name *Adonai*, I did not make myself known to them." Was God different? Did God change?

The answer is quite simple. God is God, never changing. However, people call God by different names, and the Almighty appears differently to different people. Different phases are revealed and so names of God change.

This explains why there are different religions. People tend to see God in terms of their own cultures, social systems and economic needs. From the Jewish point of view, no authentic religion is inferior or superior to another. There are simply different ways of seeing God. This is not a modern concept of tolerence but rather a Jewish idea that finds its origin in the verse below.

They worship the same God . . . though God is called by different names.

APOCRYPHA: ARISTEAS 15

76

The Hebrew Way

Judaism is not merely a way of doing, but also an all-embracing way of thinking. It demands absolute allegiance to ethical monotheism. It teaches mutual responsibility, love of all people, study as a mode of worship, benevolence, humility, justice, holiness in thought and deed. It warns against unchastity, selfishness, and all that demeans.

The most authentic term for the Jew is *ivri*, "Hebrew," from *ayver* meaning "other side," "opposite," or "apart." Abraham was called *haivri* because, as the Midrash tells us, "He was on one side, even if everyone else was on the other." Abraham did this because his sense of what life demanded of him required that he think and act differently.

For 4,000 years we have maintained a strong, cohesive culture. Judaism survived the lures of the Canaanite idolaters, the condescension of Greek thinkers, the fierce opposition of Roman emperors, the anti-Semitism of the Dark Ages, and the challenges of the modern world. We have been true to ourselves and our traditions.

I am a Hebrew and revere the God of Heaven.
                                                    JONAH 1:9

Life After Life

Nowhere in the Bible do we find specific reference to a hereafter. However, some two thousand years ago, there was a good deal of discussion about "the world to come." A book of the Talmud, *Sanhedrin*, devotes considerable thought to immortality. At one point it was controversial. Finally, belief in life after death was made an official tenet of the Jewish faith. The second blessing in the *amidah* reads, "Faithful are you in giving life to the dead. Praised are You, Lord, Master of life and death."

The next phrase is "You cause the wind to blow and the rain to fall," a line that is recited during autumn and spring. Nature dies in the fall and is revived again in the spring. The ancient rabbis reasoned that God could do the same for humans, so they proclaimed belief in "the revival of the dead." It seems highly appropriate for the Eternal People to believe fervently in immortality.

Praised are You, O God, Who grants immortality.

DAILY PRAYER BOOK

People Of The Book

In the history of the great civilizations such as Greece, Rome and Israel, only Israel had a system of literacy. Elsewhere only the upper classes and the teacher-slaves knew how to read and write. But in Israel all men knew how to read and write because of a commandment that they study Torah. Furthermore, in the year 64 the High Priest in the Temple in Jerusalem arranged a system by which every boy from age five on was to receive a Jewish education. There was always a strong disposition among the Jewish people to see that women were also instructed.

In the Middle Ages King Charlemagne could not even write his name, but almost every Jewish child could write sentences from the Torah. In this century laws for compulsory education were passed, but among the Jewish people they were enforced 1900 years ago. That the Jewish people is literate, intelligent and civilized is not a chance occurrence, but the product of a systematic commitment to learning.

And you write this teaching for yourself and also teach it to your children.

DEUTERONOMY 31:19

Safety First

During the Hadrianic persecutions the Romans forbade the teaching of Torah. They reasoned that if the Jews were restrained from studying their tradition, they would soon pass from this earth.

Rabbi Akiba ignored this law and taught Torah in public. He was warned that if he continued he would be put to death. One day, a student asked why he continued. Rabbi Akiba replied: "A fox, coming to the river's bank, suggested that the fishes might be safe from the fishermen on dry land. But the fishes replied, 'If in the water, which is our element, we are in danger, what will happen to us on the dry land?'

"So, too," continued Akiba, "if there is no safety for us in the Torah, which is our home, how can we find safety elsewhere?"

Unless we continue to teach Torah we will certainly not survive as the Jewish people. The more we learn, the more it strengthens us.

Be strong and courageous on behalf of the Torah for in it shall you obtain glory.

I MACCABEES 2:64

To Be Human Is To Differ

In the first century, two schools of thought developed: Bet Hillel and Bet Shammai. According to the Talmud, the school of Hillel generally interpreted Biblical precepts more liberally and, for the most part, its views were adopted. However, the Talmud adds: "Both are the words of the living God" (Jerusalem Talmud, Berakhot 1:7).

While the majority view was followed, Judaism recognized honest differences of opinion. The scholars who argued with great passion were friends who visited each other's homes and whose families were joined in marriage.

What an enlightened approach! These intellectual antagonists did not merely tolerate each other. They granted each other the right to dissent. Judaism recognized that laws made by majority decision must be accepted, yet minority rights are respected and freedom of conscience is assured. Judaism has always realized that human beings inevitably differ and sets a high value on individuality.

Tolerance can be based, and it will be based, on reciprocity.

THEODORE HERZL

Growing Up

The setting was Chelm, that mythical city where philosophers are fools and fools are philosphers.

Two Chelmites were engaged in earnest debate: How does one grow, from the feet up or from the head down? Said the first, "From the feet up, of course. Last year I bought my son a suit and the pants were just right. Now, they barely cover his knees. That proves that people grow from the feet up."

"Fool," snapped the second, "if you see soldiers marching, all their feet are on the same level. But their heads are at different heights. That proves that people grow from the head down."

This quaint "logic" notwithstanding, we grow from the inside out. And the Torah fosters this continuous and creative process. Education and study broaden the mind. Concern for the welfare of others develops character. Knowledge brings new insights, new maturity. In learning about others, we learn about ourselves. Intellectually, spiritually, we never stop growing.

It is essential to abiding worthy results that the process be that of a gradual slow unfolding.

LOUIS D. BRANDEIS

Learning Is The Shrine of The Jew

The greatest leader of the Jewish people was, of course, Moses. As a leader he served in many capacities. But in Jewish history he is not called a general or a liberator or a prophet but simply *Moshe Rabbaynu*, "Moses our teacher." From this, we learn that the most honored title in Judaism is teacher and the most honored activity is teaching.

From the very beginning the Jewish ideal has been to enlighten every Jew at every age of his or her life. Among the nations of antiquity the priests kept knowledge of the gods and their teachings from the masses. In Judaism knowledge was considered everybody's opportunity and responsibility.

In *The Varieties of Religious Experience* by William James, study as a form of worship is not listed. By contrast, in Judaism study is worship. Historically every synagogue was a *bet ha-midrash*, a place for learning.

Learning is the shrine of the Jew.

This book of the Torah shall not depart out of your mouth, but you shall meditate therein day and night.

JOSHUA 1:8

83

A Cluster of Grapes

Whether we are located in London, Moscow, Tel Aviv, Toronto or New York, the hearts of Jews beat as one. The rest of the world groups us together, identifies us as one people—and indeed we are.

A Midrash has an apt analogy for this belonging. It teaches that the Jewish people are like a cluster of grapes. When one grape is detached, it dries up. But when grapes cluster on the vine, they draw continual nourishment from the stock, and when pressed together they make delicious wine (Vayikrah Rabbah 36:21).

When Jews are cut off from their heritage, they find themselves withering and spiritual decay setting in. But Jews thrive when they celebrate Jewish festivals, identify with Jewish events, study the products of the fertile Jewish mind. These Jews are a flourishing branch of the glorious vintage that has enriched Judaism and civilization in every age.

This was Israel's excellence: at Sinai they were of one accord in accepting joyfully the kingdom of God. Moreover, they pledged themselves for one another.

MEKHILTA TO EXODUS 20:2

Do A Mitzvah

One of the most important and popular words in the Jewish vocabulary is *mitzvah*. *Mitzvah* is a good deed, but it is more than that. *Mitzvah* is responsibility, but it is more than that. *Mitzvah* is the proper act, but it is more than that. *Mitzvah* is derived from the Hebrew *tzavoh*, "to command" and, therefore, could also be "a command."

If *mitzvah* is a commandment, who is the commander? Moses? God? The prophets? The ancient rabbis? The Jewish tradition? The answer is: all of them. *Mitzvah* is a deep compulsion to express profound Jewish convictions. Historically, there are 613 *mitzvot;* to them should be added scores of others that are the source of Jewish thought and action. But the urge to do a *mitzvah* is weighted with the feeling that its origin is in God, that it relates to the whole universe, that it is the core of all existence. A *mitzvah* is the most important thing a Jew can do.

The whole purpose of the mitzvot is to elevate humanity.

VA'YIKRA RABBAH 13:3

A Code of Conduct

All human beings need a code of conduct. It helps to have standards to live up to. The rabbis of the Talmud picture individuals standing before the Court on High. The first question? "Did you conduct your affairs with sincerity and honesty?"

This is a dramatic illustration of the Jewish approach to life. On the Day of Judgment, we do not expect to be quizzed on doctrinal issues or articles of faith. We will be asked whether we led a decent, honorable and responsible life. The focus is not on dogma but on doing, not on professing principles of belief but on practicing loving-kindness.

Judaism has developed a systematic approach to the problems of life, and the Torah provides guidelines for every aspect of day-to-day living from interpersonal relationships to eliminating hunger and poverty.

When confronted with a challenge others ask, "What must I believe?" Jews, however, ask, "What must I do?"

All depends on deeds.

PIRKAY AVOT 3:15

The Wonder Of Words

It is not how much we say but what we say that is important. This fact is dramatized by a story in the Talmud.

Rabbi Gamaliel told one of his wise servants, "Go to the market and bring me something good." The servant brought a tongue. The rabbi then said, "Go and bring me something bad." Again the servant returned with a tongue. "A tongue, my master, may be the source of either good or evil. If it is good, there is nothing better. If it is bad, there is nothing worse."

Words are powerful. They can breed hatred or spread healing, ignite a quarrel or inspire a cause. They can trigger wars or encourage peace. Words are valuable currency and deserve to be weighed and counted rather than squandered.

The last words of the *amidah*, the Silent Devotion, reflect this: "May the words of my mouth and the meditation of my heart be acceptable to You . . . my Rock and my Redeemer."

A bird that you set free you may catch again, but a word that escapes your lips will not return.

YEHOSHUA STEINBERG

You Have To Be Taught

Who should we honor first in our society: bankers or lawyers, doctors or ditch diggers, management or labor?

Long ago the Midrash (*Pesikta De-Rav Kahana, Piska* 15) wrestled with this problem. In the third century two rabbis took a trip to a very small Jewish community, far from the center of religious life in Jerusalem. The rabbis went to the marketplace and said, "Bring to us the guardians of your city."

The people quickly brought the city council. The rabbis indicated that these were not the true guardians. Then the villagers summoned the police force but got the same response. In desperation, they asked, "Then who?"

And the rabbis said, "Bring us the teachers, for they are the true guardians of the city who protect it day and night."

Without our teachers our whole system of living and the continuity of our cultural heritage would collapse.

Let reverence for your teacher be as your reverence for God.

AVOT 4:12

88

Principles and Plans

The proclamation of the Ten Commandments is followed in the Bible by long passages of laws. In great detail they explain the everyday application of the ten basic principles of morality. Rashi, the medieval Jewish commentator, declared: "Just as the Ten Commandments were given at Sinai, so all these ordinances were given at Sinai."

Rashi knew that high ideals and great ideas are ineffective unless they take concrete form. It is pointless to talk about compassion unless we take practical steps to help the poor. The Torah urges us repeatedly to be kind to the stranger, to protect widows and orphans, to do daily deeds of lovingkindness. When we pay careful attention to "details" like these, the lofty principles take care of themselves.

God dwells in details.

ABY MORITZ WARBURG

Give Life and Get Life

Alfred Nobel made a fortune. Had he kept the profits, his name would have passed from mind. Since he used his earnings to promote prizes, his name is honored and associated with blessing.

Henrietta Szold was a great Jewish scholar. Had she been only that, she would have been a footnote in history. Because she founded Hadassah, a great humanitarian movement, her name will go down for a blessing.

Louis D. Brandeis was an outstanding corporate lawyer. Had he remained that, he would have earned vast sums. Because he was a humanitarian and served as a Supreme Court Justice, his place is secure in American history and he will be remembered for a blessing.

Individuals who convert their greatness into a life of blessing express the heart of Jewish thought, which advocates using the talents we have to benefit others. We are placed here not merely to better ourselves but "to improve the world."

How can people enhance their lives? Let them work for the welfare of people.

LEVITICUS RABBAH 25

Truth Is Where You Find It

In the classic cultures, the beginning of the world and the origin of humanity are dominated by myths and legends, tales of gods and goddesses, stories of magic and animism. But the Hebrew Bible instead focuses its attention on one supreme God, on ethical concerns and the nature of people. Adam and Eve, Abraham, Isaac, and Jacob, and Sarah, Rebecca, Rachel and Leah are portrayed as real people. They courted and married, they quarreled and reconciled, they worked hard and raised families. All their concerns were anchored in reality. The greatest emphasis of the Torah is reality.

This has guided Jewish thought through the ages—the conscious striving to reject myth, prejudice and superstition and to stress reality and truth.

No particular philosophy has absolute truth. There are many ways to view a given problem or experience, and each may be accurate. Only the sum of these views may provide the ultimate reality.

Both this view and that view are the words of the living God.

ERUVIN 13b

To Live Fully

The purpose of religion is to help us face the future and enter it in the right mood and with the proper attitude. Two Hebrew words, if translated correctly, can provide us with some excellent advice on this subject.

Toward the end of the book of Deuteronomy (30:19), as Moses concludes his great orations, he admonishes the Jewish people in the name of God, *"Uvaharta baha'yim."* This is usually translated as "Choose life." However if we wish to give full force to this phrase, we should render it "Choose to live." Commenting on these words, the sages taught that to be a complete person one needs to participate fully in life.

The coin of time is meant to be spent in quest, in worthwhile endeavors, in personal fulfillment. This does not mean withdrawing from the world or narcissism. An individual becomes a full person by enjoying life and by contributing to the lives of others.

Nothing is more precious than time and nothing so much abused.

A. SHAPIRA